AF225272

# CAPCAT

# *BLACK SHEEP*

## A Horror / Tragedy Play in Two Acts

by

## Keith Slater

## Questex

**National Library of Canada Cataloguing in Publication Data**

**Slater, Keith, author**
     **Black sheep : a horror/tragedy play in two acts / by Keith Slater.**

**(CAPCAT)**
**ISBN 978-1-896913-60-5 (paperback)**

     **I. Title.  II. Series: CAPCAT**


**PS8587.L39B63 2015          C812'.54          C2015-906244-6**

With thanks to our good friend, Liz Poulton, who sparked the germ of an idea in my mind by knitting for my wife (but ***not*** in black wool!) a garment like the one featured so prominently in this play.

# *BLACK SHEEP*

## Cast of characters

Ralph J. Barnes, a wealthy businessman  late  40's

Penny, his wife, middle 40's

Morrison, their maid, of indeterminate age

Sir Hugo Carstairs, a long-time friend, middle 40's

Sybil, his wife, middle 40's

János, a mysterious stranger, indeterminate age

Inspector Barclay, a police officer, 40's

The stranger, János, pronounces his name in his Eastern European language ("Yahnush"), indicated in the spoken text as *János*, in bold italics with the acute accent included. The English characters pronounce it as "Jaynoss," indicated by the spelling Janos.

*The action takes place in the large sitting room of the Barnes' country home in rural England, furnished with a coffee table, a few chairs and a sofa. There are two exits, one to the front door, one to a hall leading to the rest of the house and the other a French window to the garden.*

Time: the present.

ACT I Scene 1 early afternoon in late May

ACT I Scene 2 the same day, two hours later

ACT II Scene 1 a morning in early December

ACT II Scene 2 a morning in January

**ACT I, Scene 1**

*Early afternoon in late May.*

*Ralph and Penny are sitting at the coffee table.*

PENNY.  More coffee?

*No reply from RALPH.*

PENNY.  Ralph!
RALPH.  H'mm?
PENNY.  Are you listening to me?

*Still no reply.*

PENNY.  Ralph!
RALPH.  H'mm?
PENNY.  Ralph Jason Barnes!
RALPH.  Oh! The full name!
PENNY.  Are you listening to me?
RALPH.  What? Listening? Yes, of course I am!
PENNY.  Then tell me what I said.
RALPH.  What you said?
PENNY.  Yes.
RALPH.  You … er… said that …er… you were thinking of … going into town to … er … get something. A new dress, wasn't it?
PENNY.  That was ten minutes ago. I just asked if you wanted some more coffee.
RALPH.  Oh, coffee! No, thanks. Didn't you see me shake my head?
PENNY.  No, I didn't. Ring the bell for Morrison, please, will you?
RALPH.  H'mm?
PENNY.  I said … oh, never mind. I'll do it myself.

*She crosses to press a bell push.*

1

**PENNY.** Do you have to sit with your nose buried in that magazine right through lunch?

**RALPH.** Sorry. There's a really interesting article about pruning roses. He's got some new ideas I've never heard of before. He suggests alternating heavy and light pruning each time you …

**PENNY.** Spare me the details.

**RALPH.** It's not just that. He says you also have to …

**PENNY.** Ralph! I said …

***ENTER MORRISON.***

**MORRISON.** Yes, Madame?

**PENNY.** Ah, Morrison. You can clear the lunch things away now.

**MORRISON.** Yes, Madame.

**PENNY.** And we'll be having visitors for afternoon tea, remember. Sir Hugo and Lady Carstairs will be here by about three thirty.

**MORRISON.** Yes, I remembered you telling me, Madame. I've made a Victoria sponge and I thought you could offer them sandwiches – beef or ham – with cheese and biscuits first and perhaps fruit salad with cream afterwards.

**PENNY.** Yes, that sounds good. Serve it at four thirty, please.

**MORRISON.** Yes, Madame.

***MORRISON clears away the dishes through the next few minutes.***

**PENNY.** Ralph, what will you wear?

**RALPH.** Me? I've no idea. What do you suggest?

**PENNY.** I don't. You always ignore my suggestions anyway, so there's not much point in giving them to you.

**RALPH.** I'll think of something later, but first I want to concentrate on these new pruning tips. I'm going to try some of them this afternoon.

**PENNY.** You don't really have time.

**RALPH.** Yes I do. It won't take more than about an hour.

**PENNY.** That's cutting it fine. And have you done anything about the rose hedge yet? You know, where the sheep keep getting into the garden.

**RALPH.** No, not yet.

**PENNY.** Don't prune the roses in the hedge too short and make it easy for them to get in.

**RALPH.** It's just that big one, the black ram, that breaks through, then the rest follow behind.

**PENNY.** Why don't you talk to the farmer?

**RALPH.** Giles Turner? Have you ever tried talking to him? All you get is a stream of curses. And he denies it's his. Says he doesn't have a black animal in his flock.

**PENNY.** But there are no other sheep farmers for miles around.

**RALPH.** I know. That's what I said, but he threatened to stab me with a pitchfork for calling him a liar. He's tarred with the same brush as his ram!

**PENNY.** He just doesn't want to get involved in a court case for property damage.

**RALPH.** H'mm! I'm not sure. All I know is that I'm scared of that black ram.

**PENNY.** Don't be silly! It's just an animal.

**RALPH.** I've told you what happened that day I was walking back from the pub the other week.

**PENNY.** You imagined it.

**RALPH.** No! I most certainly did not!

**PENNY.** Then you must have had a few too many beers.

**RALPH.** I know what I saw.

**PENNY.** And I know what you think you saw. You've told me often enough.

**RALPH.** But you don't believe me. Anyway, I'm not thinning that hedge. I want it as dense and thorny as I can get it. Now, if I can find my pruning knife, I'll get outside and make a start on it.

**PENNY.** I've not seen it recently.

**RALPH.** No, I think it's in the potting shed. I was using it the other day. I'll go and sharpen it before I start.

***ENTER MORRISON.***

**MORRISON.** Excuse me, Madame.

**PENNY.** Yes, what is it, Morrison?

**MORRISON.** I have to pop into the village for the bread, meat and cheese. I'll be going in about an hour. I was wondering if you needed anything else.

**PENNY.** No, I don't think so, thank you.

**RALPH.** Yes, we do. Get a dozen cream cakes while you're at the bakery. Hugo was always very fond of cream cakes.

**PENNY.** Oh, yes, he was. Get a variety, all with plenty of cream. That's all we need. I think.

**MORRISON.** Yes, Madame.

***EXIT MORRISON.***

**RALPH.** Why does she always call you Madame?

**PENNY.** You tell me! I've tried time and time again to get her to call me Mrs. Barnes, or even plain Madam but no, it always has to be the whole thing, Ma-*dame*.

**RALPH.** It makes you sound very French.

**PENNY.** It makes me feel like the old senior tart in a cheap French brothel!

**RALPH.** Well I won't avail myself of your services just at the moment, thank you. My roses are waiting for me.

**PENNY.** Make sure you're back in good time. Don't forget that Hugo's bringing his new wife.

**RALPH.**  She's hardly new. They've been married for almost ten years, haven't they?

**PENNY.**  About that. I don't understand why he hasn't ever brought her to meet us before. I know he was abroad in China when they got married, but he's been back from there for over four years now and I don't think the diplomatic service works its staff all that hard, does it?

**RALPH.**  No, he wouldn't still be there if it did. Always liked his leisure time, did Hugo. Nobody could believe it when he got a First. He never seemed to do a stroke of work in the entire time we were at Cambridge together.

**PENNY.**  He must have done. You don't walk into a plum diplomatic posting unless you have something special about you.

**RALPH.**  I know. Cultural attaché to China. He must have interviewed well.

**PENNY.**  Is his wife Chinese?

**RALPH.**  Not to my knowledge.

**PENNY.**  Well, I suppose we'll find out when they get here.

**RALPH.**  I have to admit I'm not looking forward to meeting her.

**PENNY.**  Why on earth not?

**RALPH.**  I'm … not sure. I can't explain it. It's just a feeling I've got, an odd one of … fear, almost.

**PENNY.**  Fear? Her and a sheep. You seem like a bundle of psychological problems. I've never known you scared of anything before. What brought on this one?

**RALPH.**  I told you, I can't explain it. I felt funny about her as soon as I heard he was getting married.

**PENNY.**  Why?

**RALPH.**  Well, for one thing, it was so sudden. She was on the same flight as him when he had to go to some celebration of a historical discovery or something. The flight was delayed by a couple of days and they became friendly. A few weeks later, they met again at an Embassy reception and they were married within a couple of months.

**PENNY.** Sounds like a very romantic story to me.

**RALPH.** I don't think so. When he wrote to tell me about getting married to her, his letter was so vague. Kind of cagey about her. No details of her position, background, family and so on.

**PENNY.** Well, he's a man. Lots of men are like that, not saying much about their wife or girlfriend.

**RALPH.** Hugo wasn't. He was always telling me things about his current girlfriend – who her family were, where she was from, what kind of food she liked and so on.

**PENNY.** Maybe she's a very private person and asked him not to talk about her.

**RALPH.** Even to his best friend? I don't think so. I'd have been his best man at the wedding instead of the ambassador, don't forget, if he'd been married in England. And we've no idea what she looks like, because he never even sent me a wedding photograph.

**PENNY.** Yes that was a bit strange, I have to admit. I wonder why not?

**RALPH.** I've no idea. I did wonder if …

***ENTER MORRISON.***

**MORRISON.** Excuse me, Madame.

**PENNY.** Yes, what is it, Morrison?

**MORRISON.** There's a … person at the door, Madame.

**PENNY.** What do you mean, a person? What kind of person?

**MORRISON.** A very … strange one, Madame. Looking a bit like … well, a … gypsy.

**PENNY.** A gypsy? What does he want? To sell us some trash or other?

**MORRISON.** No, Madame.

**RALPH.** If he wants to do a palm reading as an excuse for begging, send him off with a flea in his ear.

**MORRISON.** No, it's not that, sir. He's given me a note for you and says it's very important.

**RALPH.** A note? Let me see it. *(She gives it to him).* Thank you.

**PENNY.** What does it say?

**RALPH.** Hang on a minute. I'm having a problem reading it. It's scrawled faintly in pencil and the handwriting's terrible. OK, here we go. 'Mr Barnes, you are in great need of my help today. I write to you that I am ready when the time is coming'. He's signed it, but I can't read his scribble. What the devil does he mean?

**PENNY.** I don't know. Get rid of him, Morrison.

**MORRISON.** Yes, Madame.

**RALPH.** And tell him I'll be calling the police if I ever see his face round here again.

### *EXIT MORRISON.*

**PENNY.** Is that all he put?

**RALPH.** Yes.

**PENNY.** No indication of what kind of help he means?

**RALPH.** No, not a hint. Here *(passing the note to her),* take a look.

**PENNY.** Yes, you're right.

**RALPH.** I know I'm right.

**PENNY.** No, wait a minute. He's signed it with your name!

**RALPH.** He's done what? Here, let me see the thing.

**PENNY.** Look, just there, in tiny letters. 'Jason'. How does he know what you're called? And why your second name? You never use it, or tell people in the village what it is, do you?

**RALPH.** No, never. But it's not 'Jason'. It's 'Janos'. See, look at it closely. That must be his name he's written, rather than mine..

**PENNY.** Oh, yes. Maybe he thinks you're kindred spirits or something.

**RALPH.** I do not have the slightest connection to any disreputable gypsy, thank you very much!

**PENNY.**  No, darling, of course you don't. I'm teasing.

**RALPH.**  Well, don't.

**PENNY.**  I'm sorry. But it's a bit funny, isn't it? Somebody with almost the same name, I mean, offering to help you in something when you don't have a clue about what you need help in.

**RALPH.**  No, it's not in the least bit funny! It's just a terrible coincidence, or somebody playing a stupid joke on me.

**PENNY.**  Who would do something like that?

**RALPH.**  How should I know? Look, can we just stop talking about it and forget the entire subject?

**PENNY.**  Yes, if you wish.

**RALPH.**  Good. I do. And now I'm going out to prune my roses.

> *EXIT RALPH through the French windows to the garden.*
>
> *PENNY picks up a magazine as the lights fade to indicate the passage of time.*
>
> *PENNY is asleep in her chair with the magazine on her lap. There is a knock on the door and she wakes up suddenly.*

**PENNY.**  What? Who's there? What is it?

> ***ENTER MORRISON.***

**PENNY.**  Oh. Morrison. It's you. I'd just dozed off for a moment. What time is it?

**MORRISON.**  It's just after three, Madame.

**PENNY.**  After three? Where's Ralph?

**MORRISON.**  I haven't seen Mr. Barnes since lunch, Madame.

**PENNY.** Oh, no! He must still be in the garden. He's not left enough time to get ready before our guests arrive.

**MORRISON.** Sir Hugo and Lady Carstairs are already here, Madame.

**PENNY.** What? Where?

***ENTER HUGO and SYBIL.***

**HUGO.** Here, Penny.

**PENNY.** Hugo! How lovely to see you again, after all these years. But you're early.

**MORRISON.** Yes, sorry. I wasn't sure how long it would take us to get here and my dear wife is a stickler about punctuality. Oh, you haven't met her before, have you?

**PENNY.** Lady Carstairs, how do you do?

**HUGO.** Oh, for heaven's sake, don't stand on formality. It's Sybil, isn't it darling?

**SYBIL.** If you wish.

**PENNY.** Oh. Yes. Well … Sybil … welcome. It's a pleasure to meet you.

**SYBIL.** Yes.

**PENNY.** That will be all for now, Morrison, thank you. You can go and continue to get the tea ready.

**MORRISON.** Yes, Madame. Would you like me to serve it earlier than planned?

**PENNY.** No, we'll still have it at four thirty.

**MORRISON.** Yes, Madame.

***EXIT MORRISON.***

**HUGO.** Right. Well, where's old Argy?

**PENNY.** Who?

**HUGO.** You know. The Argonaut.

**PENNY.** Pardon?

**SYBIL.**  Hugo, she hasn't a clue what you're talking about.

**PENNY.**  No, I'm sorry. I've no idea.

**HUGO.**  Yes! You know. R.J. Arjie. Argy. The Argonaut. Jason's ship.

**PENNY.**  Oh, you mean Ralph!

**HUGO.**  Is that what he calls himself nowadays?

**PENNY.**  It's his name.

**HUGO.**  Yes I know that, but he was always Argy at Cambridge.

**PENNY.**  Well, I've never heard of that before. Anyway, he's out in the garden. He was supposed to come in to get ready before you arrived, but …

**HUGO.**  But we got here half an hour too early, I'm sorry.

**PENNY.**  That's OK. I dropped off to sleep as well, or I'd have brought him back in.

**HUGO.**  A bit of a gardener, is he?

**PENNY.**  Yes. He was reading a magazine that had an article about …

> *There is a sudden shout of pain, followed by the bleating of a sheep in a panic-stricken state, ending abruptly.*

**HUGO.**  What the hell was that?

**PENNY.**  It sounded like Ralph shouting out in pain.

**HUGO.**  And a scared sheep.

**PENNY.**  We've been having a lot of trouble with sheep.

**HUGO.**  What kind of trouble?

**PENNY.**  Our garden backs on to the farmer's field and there's a big black ram that keeps breaking through the hedge. Ralph's really fed up with it. As soon as it's made a gap, the rest of the flock pour in behind it and trample everything down, all over the garden.

**HUGO.**  And they can do a lot of damage, I can tell you. I grew up on the family farm and we had sheep. Where one goes, the rest will soon follow.

**PENNY.**  That's right. That ram is the bane of Ralph's existence. He swears it's deliberately after him. Imagines seeing it everywhere.

**HUGO.**  Can't he complain to the farmer?

**PENNY.**  He's tried, but the farmer says it doesn't belong to him. Claims he doesn't have any black sheep in his flock.

**HUGO.**  Well, he should know. He couldn't miss a black ram.

**PENNY.**  No, you wouldn't think so, would you? Look, I think I'd better go and find out what's happened. Would you excuse me for a few minutes, please?

**HUGO.**  Yes, of course. Would you like me to come out with you?

**PENNY.**  No, it's all right, thanks. It's very muddy with all the rain we've had recently. I've got a pair of gardening boots in the shed and I won't have any problems.

**HUGO.**  Right. See you shortly.

***EXIT PENNY.***

**HUGO.**  There, you see. Nothing to be frightened about. She's nice, isn't she?

**SYBIL.**  Yes, very nice. But I'm still frightened about coming here.

**HUGO.**  I can't understand why. They're a lovely couple.

**SYBIL.**  I can't understand it either. But it's a feeling that I can't get rid of.

**HUGO.**  Yes, I know that. You've been refusing to come here with me for years now. I just wish we could work out why.

**SYBIL.**  So do I. It's a subconscious feeling, something I can't put my finger on. I don't think it's the house, or the area, or Penny. I'm scared it might be Ralph.

**HUGO.**  Old Argy? I don't think so. He wouldn't hurt a fly.

**SYBIL.**  Won't he? His wife seems happy enough. Very relaxed and comfortable. She doesn't seem to be afraid of him.

**HUGO.**  I should think not! They're a lovely couple, really well matched. We used to call them the Greek Tragedy at Cambridge.

**SYBIL.**  A tragedy? But why? I thought you said they were a lovely couple. Did something go wrong for them?

**HUGO.**  Oh, no, it was nothing like that. Although his family did kick up a bit of a fuss when they found out he was engaged to her. He'd be marrying beneath himself, they said. He became the black sheep of the family for quite a while. They were expecting him to become something big in the aristocracy. Had an earl's daughter picked out for him, whereas Penny comes from middle class stock.

**SYBIL.**  So everybody at Cambridge thought he'd done the wrong thing too, did they?

**HUGO.**  No, not at all! It was the fact that they met that was the tragedy. There must have been a dozen or more girls who had their eye on Argy and were a bit heartbroken, but it was the men around College who were really upset. Every one of them fell madly in love with Penny when they saw her. He brought her to a May Ball and they were lined up in their scores to dance, or even talk, with her.

**SYBIL.**  So what had that to do with Greece?

**HUGO.**  With Greece? Nothing. Why should … Oh, you mean the *Greek* Tragedy, of course. That was just a play on their names. You know, Jason and Penelope, straight from the pages of Greek mythology.

**SYBIL.** So people thought they were good looking, did they?

**HUGO.** Absolutely. He was like a Greek god and she was so gorgeous, really beautiful.

**SYBIL.** And you were among the trail of admirers, I suppose?

**HUGO.** What? Me? Well, I wasn't at that May Ball, so I missed the first shock impact, so to speak, but yes, I fancied her, I have to admit.

**SYBIL.** H'mm! So that's why you've been trying to get me here for all this time, is it?

**HUGO.** Oh, come on! That was almost twenty years ago.

**SYBIL.** So? She's still a very attractive woman.

**HUGO.** Look, if I would have …

**SYBIL.** Hush! I can hear somebody coming.

*Enter RALPH and PENNY. His trouser leg is torn, with blood on it and he has a pruning knife, also with blood on it, in one hand.*

**PENNY.** Look who I found, staggering back to the house.

**HUGO.** Argy! Here at last! We were just wondering … Oh! Whatever happened?

**RALPH.** I was attacked by a damned sheep, that's what happened.

**HUGO.** Attacked? By a sheep?

**RALPH.** Yes. A big ram. It was stuck in our hedge and I was trying to free it. The damned thing did its best to gore me with its horns. I just managed to dodge out of the way, so it only got a glancing scrape to my leg. It's just a scratch.

**HUGO.** That was lucky. But let me introduce my wife.

**RALPH.** Oh, yes, I'm so sorry. How rude of me to … Here, wait a minute. I know you!

**SYBIL.**  No! No, you don't!

**RALPH.**  Yes I do! We've already met.
**SYBIL.**  No, we haven't!
**RALPH.**  We have. I remember you clearly.
**SYBIL.**  You don't. It was somebody who looked like me.
**RALPH.**  No, it was you, I'm sure it was. I tell you, it was you. I remember every detail of your face and I was right next to it.
**SYBIL.**  No! You weren't! It wasn't me. I've never met you before!
**RALPH.**  Now, where was it? I'll remember it eventually. It's just there, at the back of my mind.
**SYBIL.**  It isn't, I tell you! You mustn't.
**HUGO.**  It's all right, darling. No need to get so upset.
**SYBIL.**  But he said …
**HUGO.**  I know, but it must have been somebody else. Come on, let's sit over there until you're feeling better.
**RALPH.**  *(aside)* It was her! I know it was.
**PENNY.**  Yes, darling, but leave it alone for the time being, will you?
**RALPH.**  All right, but when I remember, I'll tell her and she won't be upset when she realizes that I was right.
**PENNY.**  Yes, darling, but why don't you run upstairs and get that leg cleaned up?
**RALPH.**  It's only a scratch.
**PENNY.**  I know, but it looks such a mess. Get a wash and change out of your gardening clothes while you're up there.
**RALPH.**  Yes, OK. I'll only be a few minutes.

***EXIT RALPH.***

**PENNY.**  Are you all right, Sybil?

**SYBIL.** Yes, I'm fine, thank you. I'm sorry I made such a fuss.

**PENNY.** No, don't think about it. When Ralph gets an idea in his head, he won't let it drop, whether he's right or not. And the sheep are getting him into a real state of nerves.

**HUGO.** Why is that?

**PENNY.** It's just the one mainly. The ringleader that makes the first gap in the hedge, the big black ram, is the one that just attacked him. He claims to see it all over the place, even ones where it can't possibly be. He's been having nightmares about it recently.

**SYBIL.** Nightmares?

**PENNY.** Yes. Some of them are really bad ones, too. He'll wake up sweating.

**HUGO.** Sybil has the same problem, don't you, darling?

**SYBIL.** Yes, but the trouble is that I can never remember what they're about. If I could, I might be able to do something to stop them.

**HUGO.** They make her a nervous wreck at times.

**PENNY.** Have you had them for a long time?

**SYBIL.** It's not been that long, has it, Hugo?

**HUGO.** Not really, no. Less than a year. They originally started about six years ago, but only lasted a few weeks then. It was soon after we went on a trip to see a tomb where some ancient Chinese emperor was buried. He was reputed to use black magic of some kind to get rid of his enemies. We were there again, on a trip back to China at about this time last year and the nightmares began in earnest a few weeks later. They haven't gone away this time.

**PENNY.** Ralph's started at around the same time, but they've got worse recently.

**SYBIL.** So have mine.

**HUGO.** It was getting to the point where Sybil was turning into a recluse, scared of leaving the house. I really had to bully her to persuade her to accept your invitation to come here for tea today.

**PENNY.** Oh, dear, I'm so sorry! I hope it's not because of Ralph and me. We don't scare you, do we?

**HUGO.** No, I'm sure it's not that, is it, darling?

**SYBIL.** No, I … I don't think so.

**PENNY.** But you're not sure? Oh, how awful! But don't worry, we won't hurt you, I promise.

**SYBIL.** It's not so much the people, but something about the place.

**PENNY.** The house, do you mean? Or the village?

**SYBIL.** I don't know. But I've had the feeling for longer than the dreams.

**HUGO.** Yes, much longer. I've been trying to get her to let me ask you if we could come to see you and Ralph for a few years now, but she's always found some reason why we shouldn't visit.

**PENNY.** Oh, dear! I'm so sorry to hear that!

**SYBIL.** I'm sorry, too. But I have this feeling that terrifies me. I can't explain it, or put a finger on what it is or what it means, but every time Hugo mentioned coming here I would get this feeling of dread that just swamped my mind so I couldn't think straight.

**PENNY.** You poor thing!

**SYBIL.** It makes me feel so ashamed! I don't mean to offend you or imply …

**PENNY.** Don't worry in the least! I can understand exactly how you feel.

**SYBIL.** Thank you. You're so kind.

**HUGO.** Yes, I appreciate your attitude as well. I've felt terribly guilty about not getting in touch with you sooner. After all, Argy and I were best friends for years.

**PENNY.** Yes I know. He often tells me about … Oh, he's here now.

**PENNY.**  Well, you look a bit more presentable.

**RALPH.**  Yes, I know. I feel a lot better, too. I'm sorry about the welcome you got. You must have thought me very rude.

**HUGO.**   Don't worry about it. Penny here has been telling us all about your problems with sheep.

**RALPH.**  Yes and did she tell you it's mainly a bit black ram?

**HUGO.**  Yes, something about it following you around.

**RALPH.**   Yes, everywhere. I'll be strolling along a country lane, just out for a walk, and I'll suddenly notice a deathly silence in the hedgerows beside me. I can still hear all the usual noises – insects, birds, frogs and so on – but they're coming from a distance, not nearby.

**HUGO.**  Surely that's because they all hear you and keep quiet because they're scared?

**RALPH.**  That's what I tell myself, but it doesn't happen all the time. I can walk along the same lane on my way home, just half an hour later, and everything's normal. The usual countryside noises all round me.

**HUGO.**  It's just chance, or coincidence, or that kind of thing.

**RALPH.**  No, wait. I've not told you the worst part yet. I'll get to a little gap, where I can see through the hedge, and there's the damned ram's glowing red eyes glaring at me, filled with evil and hatred. A cold chill strikes me suddenly, right down to my bones. I get absolutely terrified, scared out of my wits. It was following me, everywhere I went, even when I was well away from the area.

**HUGO.**  It must have been a different animal.

**RALPH.**   No! Penny thought of that, but there isn't another sheep farmer for miles.

**PENNY.** Yes, I've already told them that's the case. So, did you disentangle it from the hedge?

**RALPH.** No.

**PENNY.** It got away by itself, you mean?

**RALPH.** No.

**PENNY.** So it's still there?

**RALPH.** Yes.

**PENNY.** How do you plan to get rid of it? It's going to wreck the garden when …

**RALPH.** No, it isn't. It's dead.

**PENNY.** Dead? How did it …

**RALPH.** I killed it.

**PENNY.** What?

**RALPH.** I slit its throat. When it went for me, I had the pruning knife right there, in my hand. I just dragged it across its throat, as hard and fast as I could. It stopped its bellowing at once.

**PENNY.** Yes, we heard it.

**HUGO.** Won't the farmer cause trouble for you?

**PENNY.** But he keeps saying it's not his.

**RALPH.** Yes, when I'm complaining about it wrecking my garden. You can bet he'll change his mind when he can gouge some compensation cash out of me. The boot will be on the other foot then!

**HUGO.** Will he take you to court, do you think?

**RALPH.** I don't know, but the police might.

**PENNY.** No, surely not!

**RALPH.** I think it could be a criminal offence to slaughter an animal without some kind of license.

**PENNY.** That's something else for you to have nightmares about.

**RALPH.** Yes, I'm not likely to have too many pleasant dreams in the near future, am I? It might be best if I don't ever go to sleep. I'll never get … Wait a minute!

**PENNY.** What?

**RALPH.**  That's it!

**PENNY.**  That's what?

**RALPH.**  That's how I met Sybil. It was in a dream.

**SYBIL.**  No!

**RALPH.**  Yes it was! A nightmare.

**SYBIL.**  It can't have been.

**RALPH.**  It was, I tell you! I can remember your face clearly. As soon as I saw you, I knew you straight away. And that damned ram was in the dream too. It was trying to get to you and I knew I had to save you before it did. There was some special reason why. We were in a big barn and …

**SYBIL.**  And the ram was blocking my way of escape.

**RALPH.**  Yes, it kept … How did you know that?

**SYBIL.**  I … I think I had the same dream as you. I'd forgotten all about it, but it's starting to come back now. You had a big stick and began beating it, but you couldn't get it to go out. Then you pulled a knife out of your belt and the ram seemed to …

**RALPH.**  It knew I was going to kill it if I reached it and it ran out of the barn.

**SYBIL.**  I was shivering with cold and you said I could borrow your sweater.

**RALPH.**  I took it off and …

**SYBIL.**  And put a sleeve round my neck and … I can't remember anything else.

**RALPH.**  But I can. I pulled it tight. You struggled and tried to pull it away from your throat, but I wouldn't let you escape. You were the sacrifice I had to offer to the black ram, you see. It was essential that I should be the one to do it.

**HUGO.**  So what happened next?

**RALPH.**  I don't know. I woke up in a cold sweat. And I think I only had that dream once.

***ENTER MORRISON.***

**MORRISON.**  Excuse me, sir and Madame, but that gypsy person is at the door again.

**RALPH.**  No! What does he want?

**MORRISON.**  He says to tell you that the time you need him has come.

**RALPH.**  Well, you can go and tell him that it hasn't come and it never will come, so he can just clear off and leave us alone.

**MORRISON.**  He's very persistent, sir, and quite determined to see you.

**RALPH.**  Then you need to be even more persistent and determined, Morrison, to get rid of him, don't you?

**MORRISON.**  Yes, sir.

**HUGO.**  Who is he?

**RALPH.**  Some gypsy. He was here this morning with the same kind of message.

**PENNY.**  Probably trying to sell us clothes pegs, we decided.

**RALPH.**  Or read our palms.

**PENNY.**  He thinks he's Ralph's blood brother or shadow or something.

**HUGO.**  What? Why on earth would he do that?

**RALPH.**  Because his name's vaguely similar to my second one, Jason. His is Janos.


*JÁNOS bursts suddenly into the room.*


**JÁNOS.**  Is not Janos! My name, he is *János*!


*SYBIL and PENNY both begin screaming.*


**RALPH.**  Here, steady on, old girl!

**HUGO.**  Sybil, hush now.

**HUGO.**  Come on, Sybil! Get a hold of yourself!

*It's no use.* SYBIL *won't stop.* HUGO *shakes her vigorously and finally slaps her hard across the face, but with no effect. Suddenly,* JÁNOS *steps forward, sweeps* HUGO *out of the way without touching him, and puts his palm on* SYBIL'S *forehead.*

**JÁNOS.**  Vridutz! Britzg pletork zal trovt!

*SYBIL immediately stops screaming.*

**PENNY.**  I'm so cold!

**SYBIL.**  Me too. I'm absolutely freezing!

**RALPH.**  What do you want? Get out of this house at once, or I'll phone the police!

**JÁNOS.** No.

**RALPH.**  What do you mean, no? We'll soon see whether …

**JÁNOS.**  I am telling you before now that you need me. Time is come.

**RALPH.**  Has it indeed? You can tell the police that when …

**JÁNOS.**  Is dead animal in your garden. They have interest in finding dead animal, yes?

**RALPH.**  How the hell did you know that? You can't see it from the road. You've been round the back of the house, haven't you? Trespassing!

**JÁNOS.**  *János* does not need to do this. He knows. Police will not realize is problem. Tomorrow is solved.

*EXIT JÁNOS.*

**PENNY.** Morrison, follow him and make sure he's gone.
**MORRISON.** Yes, Madame.

*EXIT MORRISON.*

**SYBIL.** Hugo, I'm so scared. And I'm shivering with cold.
**PENNY.** So'm I. What are we going to do, Ralph?
**SYBIL.** Yes, what's going to happen to us?

*The two men each hug their respective wife as the LIGHTS fade.*

**ACT I, Scene 2.**

*An evening the following September.*

**PENNY.** Isn't there a difference in Sybil?

**RALPH.** Yes, you wouldn't believe she's the same woman who was here in spring, would you? Where are they, by the way?

**PENNY.** Still in the kitchen. They insisted on clearing away the dinner things and making coffee.

**RALPH.** Couldn't Morrison have done that?

**PENNY.** Not until morning. I told her she could have an early night. She went home after serving dinner and Sybil heard me telling her she could do.

**RALPH.** They still didn't need to do the household jobs.

**PENNY.** No, but they wanted to. Sybil's like a ball of fire and she drags poor old Hugo along with her.

**RALPH.** Poor old Hugo doesn't seem to mind. Laughs at everything she makes him do.

**PENNY.** I know! Aren't they happy together?

**RALPH.** Yes, they certainly are. It's like having a couple of carefree students flitting around the house. I wish we still had that kind of energy.

**PENNY.** So do I. Oh, they're here now.

> ***ENTER SYBIL, carrying coffee things on a tray, and HUGO, opening the door for her.***

**HUGO.** I wish you'd let me carry that. It's too heavy for you.

**SYBIL.** Don't be so silly! Don't you remember the Chinese women? They did all the heavy work. I'm a beast of burden, just like them. Besides, I love to watch you open doors. There's such style and elegance in the way you do it. I could almost believe you were a gentleman.

**RALPH.** Silly!

**SYBIL.** Right, mine host and his mistress of the house. Coffee is served. Would the gentleman and lady care to place their orders for the manner in which it is to be prepared for them?

**PENNY.** Oh, Sybil, you're such a laugh! You needn't have done it, but thank you. I'll take mine black, no sugar.

**RALPH.** Black and two large spoonfuls of sugar, please.

**SYBIL.** Coming right up. Lackey, prepare the beverages, please.

**HUGO.** Yes, your munificence

**RALPH.** We were just talking about the two of you.

**SYBIL.** Aha! Do I smell the scent of gossip in this house of scandal?

**PENNY.** No, we were saying how much more relaxed you seem than you were when you came in spring.

**SYBIL.** Spring? Has it been that long?

**RALPH.** Yes, it was early May.

**HUGO.** That's right. It was just before that spy scare in the Department, and it's September now.

**SYBIL.** Of course it is. You're right, Penny. And it's true that I've felt so much better ever since then.

**HUGO.** And you've had no more nightmares.

**SYBIL.** That's right. I think you must have cured them, Ralph, by dredging the one about me getting strangled up from my subconscious.

**PENNY.** Excellent! Ralph has had far fewer as well, haven't you, darling?

**RALPH.** Yes, almost none.

**HUGO.** That's good. So our visit did lots of good all round.

**PENNY.** It certainly did.

**HUGO.** Tell me, did you have any problems with the farmer about that animal you killed?

**RALPH.** No, none at all.

**PENNY.** There was an odd incident about it, though. Tell them, Ralph.

**RALPH.** Oh, yes. Early next morning, I went to see what I should do about the thing and it had gone.

**SYBIL.** Gone?

**RALPH.** Yes. Vanished without a trace.

**PENNY.** Not even a sign of any blood or bits of wool on the thorns.

**RALPH.** It hadn't rained, so I thought somebody must have taken the dead animal away, then trimmed the hedge and hoed the ground. You couldn't tell, though.

**HUGO.** And the farmer really never said or did anything?

**RALPH.** No, not a thing.

**PENNY.** He's never been friendly since Ralph first complained about his flock breaking into our garden, but he didn't get any more unfriendly.

**SYBIL.** You wouldn't buy from him, though, would you?

**RALPH.** Well …

*A pause.*

**SYBIL.** What? Don't tell me you bought that delicious lamb you served for dinner from him!

**PENNY.** Er … not exactly.

**RALPH.** It wasn't lamb. It was mutton.

**HUGO.** What? Don't be ridiculous!

**RALPH.** It was. And very old mutton, too.

**HUGO.** Oh, come on! Don't forget that I grew up on a sheep farm. That was the tastiest, most tender lamb I've ever had in my entire life.

**RALPH.** I've no idea whether it was or it wasn't, but what we served was mutton several years old.

**HUGO.** I don't believe you.

**SYBIL.** Neither do I.

**RALPH.** It's true.

**HUGO.** You can't be serious.

**RALPH.**  I can and I am. That meat was from the black ram I killed in our garden.

**SYBIL.**  No! Don't say that!

**RALPH.**  It's true. Tell them, Penny.

**PENNY.**  Yes, it is. A few weeks after you were here, there was a knock at the door and it was that gypsy, Janos. He had some big cardboard boxes and they were full of meat, all butchered, frozen and wrapped up in black paper with the content written on the package.

**SYBIL.**  Black paper? That seems very odd.

**PENNY.**  Yes, we thought so, too. We'd never seen paper like it. Absolutely pitch black, smooth and glossy all over. It's hard to describe.

**SYBIL.**  Does it mean anything, do you think?

**PENNY.**  No, of course not!

**RALPH.**  We tried to refuse it, but he said it was ours, so we must take it.

**PENNY.**  Then we tried to pay him for butchering the animal, but he wouldn't take any money.

**RALPH.**  He said all he wanted was the head and would we mind if he took it?

**PENNY.**  We told him that was fine. He said he'd assumed it would be all right and not put it in the freezer with the rest of the meat.

**RALPH.**  It must have been pretty rank by that time.

**HUGO.**  Yes, and definitely not exactly gourmet quality by now!

**RALPH.**  You could have it stuffed and mounted on the wall like a hunting trophy.

**HUGO.**  You'd want the eyes taken out so it wasn't looking accusingly at you the whole time.

**RALPH.**  Well, you could give them to somebody from those Middle Eastern countries that regard them as a culinary treat.

**HUGO.**  You'd need a few more to make a decent sized meal. And some other kinds of food to fill the plate.

**SYBIL.**  Please could we change the subject?

**HUGO.** We're just having a joke.

**SYBIL.** It might be a joke to you, but I don't find it funny.

**HUGO.** You usually have a good sense of humour.

**PENNY.** Hugo, she's upset. Can't you both see? She's trembling.

**RALPH.** Are you all right, Sybil?

**SYBIL.** No.

**HUGO.** What is it, darling? What's wrong?

**SYBIL.** I've got that horrible feeling again, the one I used to have when I woke up from one of my nightmares.

**HUGO.** But you've not had one of those for ages.

**SYBIL.** I know, but I've got the same feeling now. And I feel so cold! I'm freezing. Absolutely freezing!

**RALPH.** She's shivering. It's shock.

**PENNY.** I've got the shivers as well. I've gone really chilly.

**RALPH.** Why don't you both sit down? Let's put our jackets round them, Hugo, and I'll get a couple of brandies for them.

***RALPH and HUGO busy themselves with attending to the two women.***

**PENNY.** Let's talk about something else, something more pleasant. Tell us how you met Hugo, please, won't you, Sybil?

**SYBIL.** It was on a flight. Hugo had boarded at Heathrow, on the way to start his new job in Beijing. I'd been to Bahrain to visit my sister, who was living in the Middle East at the time, and got on the same plane when it landed there.

**HUGO.** That's right. Then there was some kind of mechanical defect and we had to land in Singapore. We were stuck there for three days before they got the parts flown in and fixed the problem.

**SYBIL.** There was something wrong with my passport – they said it wasn't my picture – but Hugo arranged things so I could leave the airport and get a hotel room.

**RALPH.** Very gallant of you, Hugo.

**HUGO.** Not really. As far as I knew, she was just a British citizen with a problem and, as a diplomat, it was my duty to help her.

**RALPH.** Yes, we believe you, of course, but I'll bet you wouldn't have been quite as efficient at the task if she hadn't been an attractive young woman.

**HUGO.** I think I would. I'd not been a diplomat all that long and I was keen to …

**SYBIL.** Darling, Ralph's teasing you.

**HUGO.** What? Oh. Is he? Sorry.

**SYBIL.** Anyway, he was very attentive to me all the time we were stuck in Singapore and on the flight when the plane was fixed.

**PENNY.** So is that when you started going out together?

**HUGO.** No I, had to rush off as soon as we landed. The Embassy car was sitting there with the driver looking for me. Some kind of minor emergency and the delay had made things worse.

**SYBIL.** We didn't meet again for almost a year.

**HUGO.** I'd no idea where she worked or lived and she was too embarrassed to contact me.

**SYBIL.** That wasn't the kind of thing a well-brought-up girl did.

**HUGO.** I was kicking myself for not asking her how I could get in touch.

**SYBIL.** Then I was invited to an Embassy party and I was sitting there when Hugo walked in, looking as if he was bored to death.

**HUGO.** That's because I was bored to death.

**SYBIL.** I recognized him straight away, but I didn't expect him to remember me.

**HUGO.** I knew her at once. My boredom instantly vanished.

**SYBIL.** He came straight over to me with a big grin plastered all over his face. I was so happy!

**HUGO.** And that's how it all began. We were married six months later.

**PENNY.** Oh, what a lovely story! It's so romantic, isn't it, Ralph?

**RALPH.** Yes, very nice.

**RALPH.** She was the most exciting, vivacious person I'd ever met.

**SYBIL.** Not for long, though, was it?

**HUGO.** No. I think I mentioned a bit about it in a letter, Ralph.

**RALPH.** You said Sybil was having nervous trouble, but without going into details.

**PENNY.** What exactly was the problem, Sybil? The nightmares?

**SYBIL.** Not at that point, no. I was convinced that I was being followed. Everywhere I went, I could feel somebody's eyes on me, watching every move I made. There was no reason why anybody should be interested in me. Hugo wasn't involved in cloak and dagger stuff and I certainly wasn't. It got to the point where I couldn't go out in public without being so terrified that I literally went into shivering fits.

**PENNY.** Oh, how awful for you!

**HUGO.** Yes, but it got worse. Tell them, darling.

**SYBIL.** Yes, it did. I reached the stage where I began to feel the same terror even when I was in our own home.

**PENNY.** And do you still have the same problem?

**SYBIL.** No, it's so strange, but it stopped at the same time as the nightmares did, after we came to visit you.

**RALPH.** That's excellent! We could advertise our house as a health clinic where nervous disorders are cured.

**PENNY.** Ralph, don't be silly! But, seriously, you must pay us a visit whenever you can.

**HUGO.** We will, yes. It did me good to see how coming here cured Sybil when none of a dozen doctors we'd

consulted had a clue about what to do. They told her that
she had a serious mental illness and wanted to shove her in
an asylum.

**RALPH.** Well, you're welcome here any time and we
won't put you on drugs or shock treatment, we promise,
don't we, Penny?

**PENNY.** Yes, of course! And we're having a party in
early December to celebrate our twentieth anniversary. I've
got you down on the guest list and I'll be sending the
invitations out next week. Keep the date free. Second
Saturday of the month.

**HUGO.** I don't know. The weather might be a problem,
driving home late at night. It's a three-hour journey.

**RALPH.** We'd thought of that. We're putting you in the
guest room for the night. Everybody else is local, so it
won't be any trouble.

**HUGO.** Look, didn't you tell us you're going off for a
holiday over Christmas and the New Year? You don't want
us getting in the way when you have to pack and get ready.

**PENNY.** You won't make any difference. We've ten
days after the party until we set off.

**HUGO.** Well, I don't know. It might …

**SYBIL.** Oh, let's say yes, Hugo! We've not had much of
a social life with all my illness. It will be wonderful to
spend a weekend in a place where I feel so safe.

**HUGO.** Yes, I have to admit that it's wonderful to see
how happy and relaxed you are here. All right. We're
delighted to accept and we'll plan to arrive at about …

*The French windows suddenly burst open and
JÁNOS ENTERS. He is carrying a parcel. SYBIL
begins to scream. JÁNOS points to her and speaks.*

**JÁNOS.** Vridutz!

*SYBIL'S scream is immediately silenced.*

**RALPH.** What do you mean by coming in here like that?

**JÁNOS.** Is nobody to answering when I go to front of house.

**RALPH.** That doesn't give you the right to come into our back garden. That's trespassing. It's against the law. I could take you to court for it.

**JÁNOS.** How do I come into house other way if nobody let me come into front door of house?

**RALPH.** You don't. You only come in if you're invited to come in. Who the devil do you think you are?

*JÁNOS throws his head back and laughs sardonically, but doesn't speak.*

**RALPH.** Come on! Who are you?

**JÁNOS.** I am *János*.

**RALPH.** I know what you say you're called, but who are you? What are you? Why did you crash into our house like that?

**JÁNOS.** I come to give what is yours.

**PENNY.** What do you mean, ours?

*JÁNOS hands the parcel to SYBIL, who opens it. It contains a garment knitted from black wool.*

**SYBIL.** What is it?

**PENNY.** It's a sort of … narrow shawl, maybe, or … no, it's more like a wide scarf, but it's got sleeves knitted into it at each end.

**RALPH.** It's not ours.

**JÁNOS.** Yes, is yours! Is from black sheep I am taking from your garden. You remember, you cut throat of sheep when …

**RALPH.** I know, I know! All right!

PENNY.  But … how did the fleece turn into this? Who did the work and knitted it into this … shawl?

JÁNOS.  Is my woman. She is knowing from many time ago how to spin fleece into yarn and knit to make garment.

RALPH.  Then we have to pay you for her time and effort.

JÁNOS.  No, is OK. But if you permit there is other wool still to change into yarn. Please may I keep this? My woman is to make scarf for me.

RALPH.  Yes, that's fine. We don't need it. In fact, we didn't even want this … thing.

PENNY.  Ralph, don't be so rude. It's lovely. Please tell your … wife we think it's a lovely gift and we really thank her for making it.

JÁNOS.  Yes I tell this to her. And I thank you that you give me all other wool.

PENNY.  You're very welcome.

JÁNOS.  Is good. I leave now.

*JÁNOS EXITS quickly through the French windows.*

RALPH.  Hang on! You can leave by the proper …

*He is too late. JÁNOS has left. RALPH rushes across to the French windows.*

RALPH.  I said you can … oh, he's vanished.
HUGO.  Vanished? How?
RALPH.  I've no idea, but he's gone.
HUGO.  He can't have gone. There wasn't enough time.
RALPH.  Well, he's not here. See for yourself.

*HUGO crosses to the French windows.*

**HUGO.**  You're right. I can't believe it.

**SYBIL.**  Hugo, I'm scared!

**HUGO.**  It's OK, darling. He's gone.

**SYBIL.**  It's not OK! I'm getting that horrible fear again.

**PENNY.**  Try not to think about him, Sybil.

**RALPH.**  I'll go to see the police about him in the morning. Get them to find where he's camping and move him and the rest of his gypsy band out of the area.

**PENNY.**  Let's try on this thing he brought. The shawl or scarf or whatever it is.

*PENNY puts the garment on.*

**PENNY.**  Oh, it's lovely! So warm! Just the thing for keeping me warm when the cold weather gets here in winter.

**RALPH.**  It doesn't look all that bad on you.

**PENNY.**  It feels very cosy.

**SYBIL.**  Yes, it looks as if it would be.

**PENNY.**  It's a bit too hot to wear indoors, but it will be just the thing on a chilly night. Here, Sybil, try it on.

*PENNY takes off the shawl and passes it to SYBIL, who has some difficulty in putting it on.*

**SYBIL.**  There! That's got it! Oh, yes, it's lovely and warm, isn't it?

**PENNY.**  Yes, and it looks good on you.

**SYBIL.**  I wouldn't mind one of these myself. I wonder if there's a knitting pattern for it?

**PENNY.**  I'm sure there will be. Is there a yarn shop near where you live?

**SYBIL.**  Yes, not far from our house. I'll look for one when I have time to do some knitting.

**PENNY.**  What colour will you use?

**SYBIL.** I'm not sure. Red, maybe. Something bright to cheer me up in winter.

**PENNY.** Yes, red will suit you well.

**SYBIL.** It's making me feel too hot. I need to take it off.

***SYBIL struggles to remove the shawl, but can't get free of it and begins to panic.***

**SYBIL.** It … won't … come off. It's stuck! It's got me … trapped! Help me, somebody, please! It's strangling me!

**HUGO.** Steady on, old girl! Here, just stop struggling while I get your arms out.

***He does so, but with difficulty.***

**HUGO.** There, that's got it.

**SYBIL.** Thank you. I was beginning to feel scared. You know, like I used to be after those nightmares.

**HUGO.** Well, there's no need to be. You only got a bit stuck. All it needed was just somebody to give you a hand.

**SYBIL.** Yes, I was being a bit silly, wasn't I?

**HUGO.** A little, yes.

**PENNY.** No, you weren't. I was scared half out of my wits when he burst in like that and I've never had all the nervous stress you've been through.

**RALPH.** I agree and I'm going to do something about it.

**HUGO.** What can you do?

**RALPH.** I told you, I'll go to the police station tomorrow and find out how we can get rid of this damned gypsy and his band of thugs.

**PENNY.** I think they're called travellers these days, darling.

**RALPH.** Are they? Well, they'd better start travelling, then, hadn't they? And then they can go on travelling until they've travelled clear out of the county! Now, how about another drink? Sybil? Dessert wine? Brandy?

**SYBIL.**  Not for me, thanks.

**RALPH.**  Hugo? What about you?

**HUGO.**  Not for me either. I think it's about time we were making tracks. It will be after eleven by the time we get home.

**RALPH.**  It's Saturday. You don't need to get up early tomorrow.

**HUGO.**  I do, actually. I have to make an early start on planning a conference tomorrow, weekend or not.

**SYBIL.**  And you must come to visit us soon.

**PENNY.**  That would be lovely!

**SYBIL.**  I'll phone you to arrange things.

**RALPH.**  Well, if I can't talk you into one for the road, I'll wish you a safe journey.

**PENNY.**  Yes and don't forget you're coming for the weekend in December.

**HUGO.**  We won't.

**SYBIL.**  No, we won't forget. We'll be here, gypsy or no gypsy, nightmares or not!

***LIGHTS.***

## ACT II, Scene 1

*A morning in early December.*

*RALPH, PENNY, HUGO and SYBIL are sitting round the coffee table.*

**PENNY.** Morrison will be here with the coffee in a few minutes.

**SYBIL.** Lovely.

**HUGO.** Nothing like a good cup of coffee after a delicious lunch. The perfect end to a perfect weekend.

**SYBIL.** Yes, it was lovely to relax after dinner last night, instead of having to drive home.

**HUGO.** It certainly was! The wind was really violent yesterday. Even though the snowstorm didn't get this far south, it wouldn't have been a pleasant trip back. To make things worse, the car heater doesn't seem to be working properly.

**RALPH.** I know how you feel about not enjoying late night travel. We had the same feeling of relief when we stayed overnight on our weekend with you last month.

**PENNY.** Yes, isn't it a treat to loaf around on the Sunday morning after a good night's sleep?

**SYBIL.** It certainly is.

**RALPH.** How's that delightful cat of yours?

**HUGO.** Tumkins? Oh, he's fine.

**PENNY.** Do you have to put him in a cat place when you go away for the weekend?

**SYBIL.** No, we have a cat-sitter, a student who lives nearby and comes in to see to him a few times each day. She loves cats and the money we give her is useful for her, too.

**RALPH.** There's nothing not to love about him. I've never seen a friendlier cat.

**PENNY.** Yes, particularly when he's a Persian. Aren't they supposed to be very vicious?

**SYBIL.** Many of them are, but not Tumkins. He's never been nasty in the three years we've had him.

**RALPH.** I've always been a dog lover myself. Good company on long walks out here in the country.

**HUGO.** I didn't know you had a dog.

**PENNY.** We don't at the moment. Our last one, a black Lab, had to be put down in spring when he got sick. Liver problems. We plan on looking for another one in the New Year, when we get back from our holiday. Most of our neighbours have dogs.

**SYBIL.** Your neighbours seem to be very nice people. The ones who were here last night did, at least.

**PENNY.** Yes, they are. We like them and they're good friends.

**RALPH.** They are. Terry Sewell can be a bit of a bore at times, but he's a good soul at heart.

**PENNY.** Ralph! Don't say such horrible things!

**RALPH.** Well, he does keep going on about football. He's got no other conversation.

**HUGO.** We have a couple of chaps in our Section who're just the same. George Latimer and Henry Vale. Remember George from Cambridge, Ralph?

**RALPH.** Latimer? No, I don't think so.

**HUGO.** You must do. Into the Occult in a big way.

**RALPH.** Ah, yes, vaguely. Is he still interested in that sort of thing?

**HUGO.** No, I don't think so. Anyway, he and Henry are both loyal Chelsea fans. They'll be going on about yesterday's game when I see them tomorrow morning.

**RALPH.** Chelsea? Terry was talking about that game last night. Against Manchester United, I think. Some kind of key match for top of the league at the Christmas mid-season mark, wasn't it?

**HUGO.** That's right. What was the result, did he say?

**RALPH.** Three – two, I believe, but I don't remember which way round. A last-minute winning goal. Look, the Sunday Times has arrived. Here, check up on it for yourself.

**HUGO.**  I will, thanks, then I can join in the discussion in the office tomorrow.

**PENNY.**  Ah, here's Morrison with the coffee.

### *ENTER MORRISON.*

**MORRISON.**  Coffee, Madame.

**PENNY.**  Thank you. Morrison is the culinary genius who did wonders for the party last night.

**SYBIL.**  Really? It was excellent, Morrison. You performed miracles.

**MORRISON.**  Thank you, your ladyship.

**PENNY.**  She always does. That's all for just now, Morrison.

**MORRISON.**  Thank you, Madame.

### *EXIT MORRISON.*

**RALPH.**  Did you find the game, Hugo?

**HUGO.**  Yes and it sounds like an exciting one.

**RALPH.**  Was I right about the score?

**HUGO.**  You were, but Chelsea lost. They were two-nil up at half-time, but Manchester got two early in the second half. Then they scored the winner in the last minute of stoppage time. George and Henry must have been devastated.

**RALPH.**  A pity George couldn't call on witchcraft or evil spirits or whatever he used to have, and cast a spell on United.

**HUGO.**  Yes, isn't it? I'll tell him that if they go on moaning for too long.

**SYBIL.**  Does Morrison do all your cooking?

**PENNY.**  Pretty well all of it. Lunch and dinner anyway. We fend for ourselves at breakfast unless we have guests. That's why she was here this morning.

**SYBIL.**  You're lucky to have her.

**PENNY.** Yes, aren't we? She's a treasure. And she really enjoys doing it. She hasn't much else in life and the money's useful as well, of course. She'll do just about anything I ask.

**SYBIL.** That must be wonderful.

**PENNY.** Yes, it is. This weekend, for instance, I asked her to make sure she didn't serve any of that meat Janos – sorry, *János*, I should say – brought for us. I was concerned that it might bring back unpleasant memories for you.

**HUGO.** That was kind of you, thanks, but I don't think it would have caused a problem.

**SYBIL.** No, I think I'm cured of my difficulties.

**HUGO.** What happened about that sheep? And is there anything new on the disappearing gypsy?

**RALPH.** No. It's the strangest thing. I got in touch with the police but they'd never heard of him. There are no records of any gypsies – sorry, travellers – anywhere in the area. None for miles around. They claimed they did a search when I insisted but drew a complete blank. I got the impression that they were just giving me a condescending little pat on the head.

**SYBIL.** The whole thing's really odd, isn't it?

**HUGO.** It certainly is. You don't want suspicious characters like that wandering all over your property.

**PENNY.** No, especially as we go off for a month's holiday next week.

**SYBIL.** Lucky you! Where are you going?

**PENNY.** We fly to the Azores for a week, then cruise from there to the Caribbean, spend ten days in Barbados, then fly back home in mid-January.

**SYBIL.** How lovely! Unfortunately, Hugo's too busy for us to get away just now.

**HUGO.** And for the foreseeable future. It's the immigrant problem that's keeping us so busy. I was lucky to get this weekend freed up.

**RALPH**. I don't suppose you can stay another night, then, can you? The weather's getting worse.

**HUGO.** No, sorry, although it would have been a great pleasure. But I checked the forecast in the Sunday Times and it's not supposed to get really bad until the late evening. We'll have to be getting off quite soon.

**RALPH.** How are you for petrol? The first service station on the M4 is about forty miles away and nothing's open round here on Sunday afternoon.

**HUGO.** We've plenty. I filled up there on the way here. Our only problem is the dodgy car heater.

**RALPH.** Shall we take a look under the bonnet?

**HUGO.** Not in this weather. We'd freeze. No, we're in for a cold journey, I'm afraid.

**PENNY.** Sybil, why don't I lend you that shawl with sleeves? You know, the one that gypsy gave me.

**SYBIL.** Oh, I don't know. You'll need it yourself in this weather.

**PENNY.** No, I've got other things.

**RALPH.** And she won't need it in the places we'll be going to next week for a month.

**PENNY.** That's right. Go on. Borrow it. It's really warm.

**HUGO.** We can send it back in the post tomorrow.

**PENNY.** No, don't bother. Use it while we're away. You can bring it back next time you come to visit. By the time we get back from our holiday the weather should be starting to warm up, so I won't need it again this winter.

**SYBIL.** It's tempting, but … I'm a bit worried about what happened the last time I put it on.

**PENNY.** The panic attack, you mean?

**SYBIL.** Yes.

**HUGO.** But it wasn't anything serious. You were fine as soon as I gave you a hand.

**SYBIL.** Yes. Yes, I was, wasn't I? I was just being silly, wasn't I?

**HUGO.** Yes, of course you were! Although you'd been going through a rough time with that spell of nightmares as well, don't forget.

**SYBIL.** Yes, that was the biggest problem, wasn't it? All right, Penny, I'll borrow it, please. And I'll wear it again in bad weather if you're sure you don't mind.

**PENNY.** No, of course I don't. Come on, we'll go upstairs and get it.

**HUGO.** I'll come with you to get our bag down, then bring the car to the front door.

> *PENNY, SYBIL, HUGO and RALPH EXIT. The LIGHTS dim. MORRISON ENTERS and clears away the coffee things, then the LIGHTS go briefly to black to indicate the passage of time. When the LIGHTS rise again, PENNY and RALPH are sitting reading. She has a magazine and he has the Sunday Times.*

**PENNY.** Will they be home yet?

**RALPH.** Pardon?

**PENNY.** Sybil and Hugo. Will they have got home yet?

**RALPH.** Home? Oh. How long since they left? A couple of hours?

**PENNY.** Yes, about that.

**RALPH.** Then no, they can't be anywhere near home yet. At least another hour. More if there are traffic problems.

**PENNY.** I hope they're all right.

**RALPH.** Yes.

**PENNY.** They must be freezing in that car without a heater.

**RALPH.** They're probably fine. The temperature's still a few degrees above zero.

**PENNY.**  The wind's blowing fairly hard, though.

**RALPH.**  Yes, but I don't think it's quite as bad as it was yesterday.

***ENTER MORRISON.***

**MORRISON.**  Excuse me, Madame.

**PENNY.**  Yes, Morrison, what is it?

**MORRISON.**  There's a gentleman here, asking to see the master.

**RALPH.**  A gentleman? What kind of gentleman? And what does he want?

**MORRISON.**  He didn't say, sir, but I think he could be a policeman.

**RALPH.**  A policeman?

**MORRISON.**  Yes, sir. He called himself inspector something-or-other, but he didn't look like the kind of inspector that checks for faulty drains or gas leaks and things like that.

**RALPH.**  Why would the police want to see me?

**PENNY.**  I've no idea, but there's a simple way to find out and we can't leave him standing on the doorstep. Ask him to come in and show him into here, Morrison.

**MORRISON.**  Yes, Madame.

***EXIT MORRISON.***

**RALPH.**  It must be about that black sheep.

**PENNY.**  Do you think so? After all this time?

**RALPH.**  Yes. I knew I'd be in trouble about it some day. The farmer must have reported it.

**PENNY.**  But why did he take so long to complain?

**RALPH.**  I've no idea. Maybe he was checking his flock for some reason and noticed it was missing. Or maybe he only just found out that I'd killed it.

**PENNY.**  Who would have known?

**RALPH.** I don't know and I don't suppose we'll ever find out. The police are very cagey about these things.

**PENNY.** Hush! He's here.

***ENTER MORRISON and BARCLAY, who shows his warrant card.***

**BARCLAY.** Good afternoon. Detective Inspector Barclay, of the county police force.

**PENNY.** Do come in and sit down. Would you like some tea?

**BARCLAY.** Please. I never say no to a nice cuppa.

**PENNY.** Good. Morrison, would you make tea, please? And bring some of those chocolate biscuits you bought the other day.

**MORRISON.** Yes, Madame.

***EXIT MORRISON.***

**RALPH.** Now, what was it you came about, inspector?

**BARCLAY.** Well, now, I believe you reported a strange person trespassing in your back garden recently.

**RALPH.** Yes, I did, but I'd hardly call it recently.

**BARCLAY.** I'd like to ask you a few questions about it, if I may.

**RALPH.** Of course, but why did it take you so long to get round to it?

**BARCLAY.** Oh, you know, sir, pressure of work. We've had a spate of more serious crimes recently.

**PENNY.** You didn't believe what Ralph said, did you?

**BARCLAY.** I wouldn't go that far, madam.

**PENNY.** But you thought he was exaggerating.

**BARCLAY.** Just a little, maybe. To be honest, we wondered if some practical joker had been playing tricks and taken you both in.

**RALPH.** So why the questions now, all of a sudden? What changed your mind?

**BARCLAY.** An unusual incident that happened a few days ago.

**PENNY.** What kind of incident?

**BARCLAY.** You'll appreciate that I can't give you any details, but the incident was similar to the one you reported. A strange man was in their back garden, but had completely vanished by the time they'd opened the door to ask him what he was up to. When they checked, he'd left an animal behind.

**RALPH.** An animal? Was it a sheep?

**BARCLAY.** A sheep? No, sir, it was a chicken. What made you think it might have been a sheep?

**RALPH.** Oh, there was one … involved in our case. I thought you might have heard about it.

**BARCLAY.** How would I have heard about it?

**RALPH.** From the farmer. When you arrived, I thought it was because he'd reported it.

**BARCLAY.** Reported what, sir?

**RALPH.** That it was missing. You see, there was this sheep that kept breaking through our hedge and leading a lot more into the garden, trampling all the plants. One day, it got stuck in the hedge and I was trying to release it by cutting it free with my pruning knife, but it slipped and I … accidentally … caught the animal's throat when it … nudged my hand and it started bleeding a lot and … died.

**BARCLAY.** I see. We've had no reports of anything like that, sir. But I can check again. Though accidents with sheep don't always get reported unless there's any unusual features.

**RALPH.** This one was unusual. The animal was a big ram and jet black.

**BARCLAY.** Black?

**RALPH.** Yes. Is that important?

**BARCLAY.** It could be. The chicken he left behind was unusually big, see. And it was described as coal black.

**PENNY.** The ram was completely black, right through every fibre. You could see that in the shawl.

**BARCLAY.** Which shawl?

**RALPH.** That's how it ended. He started off by coming to the door and leaving us a message that we needed him.

**BARCLAY.** Did he say why?

**RALPH.** Not at that point, no. But later on, after I'd … after the … incident with the sheep, he suddenly burst into the room. We had friends visiting us – Sir Hugo and Lady Carstairs – and we were all shocked.

**PENNY.** Sybil and I were terrified!

**RALPH.** He said the time for his help had come and offered to get rid of the carcass for us. It had vanished without a trace next morning.

**PENNY.** Then, a few weeks later, he came back.

**RALPH.** Hugo and Sybil were here once more and we all got scared again.

**PENNY.** He told us his wife – his woman, he called her, so maybe they weren't married – anyway, she'd knitted this kind of a shawl with sleeves in it for me.

**RALPH.** He insisted that we had to take it and wouldn't accept a penny.

**PENNY.** Sybil said it was called a nightingale.

**BARCLAY.** Would you mind if I took a look at it?

**RALPH.** Not at all, but you've just missed it.

**PENNY.** Hugo and Sybil were visiting over the past weekend and I lent it to her this morning to keep her warm on the way home. Oh, here's the tea.

***ENTER MORRISON with a tea tray. She begins to serve everybody.***

**PENNY.** Thank You, Morrison.

**BARCLAY.** It's a pity the shawl isn't still here. It would have been useful to compare something he'd left here with the chicken at the other place.

**RALPH.** What about the meat? Would that do?

**BARCLAY.** What meat?

**RALPH.**  He butchered the animal and gave it to us, all nearly packaged. In unusual paper. It was black.

**BARCLAY.**  Black? Yes, I'd certainly like to take a look at that. I only need a fairly small amount. Maybe just one package.

**PENNY.**  Of course, inspector. Morrison, would you bring a package of the lamb from the freezer, please?

**MORRISON.**  Yes, Madame.

*EXIT MORRISON.*

**RALPH.**  What's the meat going to tell you, inspector?

**BARCLAY.**  I can't honestly say, sir. I'll just hand it over to Forensics. You'd be amazed at the miracles they can pull off. Fingerprints, of course, or DNA from where he touched the paper. The sort of blade used to cut the meat. All kinds of interesting things.

**PENNY.**  Maybe they can explain why the skin of the meat is black.

**RALPH.**  Yes, we thought it had got stained from the wrapping paper, but it hadn't. It wouldn't wash off and, besides, it was only the outside of the meat that was black. The rest of it was the normal red colour, even though the paper had been in the same contact with it.

**BARCLAY.**  So the skin was noticeably black, was it?

**PENNY.**  Yes, as black as coal.

**RALPH.**  I was talking to Hugo about it. He said he'd never come across anything like it and he grew up on his dad's sheep farm.

**BARCLAY.**  I think the forensic results from that meat will be extremely interesting.

**PENNY.**  Really? Why, particularly?

**BARCLAY.**  Because the children had been in a fight that had pulled a few feathers out and the skin you could see was black too, not the usual whitish colour.

**RALPH.**  So it seems there could be …

**MORRISON.** Oh, Mrs. Barnes! Mrs. Barnes!

**PENNY.** Morrison! Whatever is wrong?

**MORRISON.** Mrs. Barnes, madam – I mean Madame, I'm sorry – it's gone!

**RALPH.** Come on, pull yourself together, girl! What's gone?

**MORRISON.** The meat, sir. Every bit of it.

**PENNY.** You mean the entire freezer full?

**MORRISON.** No, just the lamb. Every package of it.

**RALPH.** Are you sure?

**MORRISON.** Certain, sir. You can't miss that black wrapping paper. And all the other meat in the freezer wasn't touched. There was some good cuts of beef, too.

**PENNY.** I'm sorry, inspector, but we can't let you have anything of use that he left behind.

**BARCLAY.** Yes, I can see that. So I don't think there's much more that I can do here just now. Would you be kind enough to get in touch with me when your friends return that shawl, please?

**RALPH.** We will, yes.

**BARCLAY.** Thanks. I'll be on my way, then.

**RALPH.** Good bye, inspector. And best of luck with your enquiries.

**BARCLAY.** Thank you, sir.

**MORRISON.** I'll see the gentleman out, Madame.



**PENNY.** Now what?

**RALPH.** What do you mean, now what?

**PENNY.** We were talking about Hugo and Sybil before that policeman arrived.

**RALPH.** Were we?

**PENNY.** Yes. Wondering if they'll get home safely in that car, with its broken heater.

**RALPH.** They'll be fine. Sybil has your shawl if she gets cold.

**PENNY.** I know. And I have a bad feeling about that, after what the inspector said.

**RALPH.** I have as well. It's a bit worrying, isn't it?

**PENNY.** Then there's this weather. Will they come to any harm in it?

**RALPH.** Let's hope not. Several people died in the storm, it says in the paper.

**PENNY.** Really?

**RALPH.** Yes, but most of them were up North, where they had heavy snowfalls as well. There were just two fatalities down South, one in the New Forest when a tree fell on a man and a traffic accident in London. A woman who got dragged off her feet by a passing car.

**PENNY.** Oh, that's terrible!

**RALPH.** Yes it was a freak accident. She was waiting for the lights to change at a crosswalk as a car went past. She was wearing a long scarf and it got caught in the car wheels. She was dragged along for a fair distance before the driver realized she was there and she was strangled to death by the time anybody reached her. She was apparently quite a well-known designer. It says that she's … hang on!

**PENNY.** What is it?

**RALPH.** What were the names of those men that Hugo mentioned?

**PENNY.** Which men?

**RALPH.** You know, the two who were keen Chelsea fans?

**PENNY.** I can't remember.

**RALPH.** Was one of them George Latimer?

**PENNY.** Yes, I think it was. Why?

**RALPH.** Listen to this. 'The victim was Lady Latimer, the well-known British fashion designer, who recently created a stir at the International World Haute Couture

Assembly in New York with her radical black and white stark clothing collection '.

**PENNY.** What about it?

**RALPH.** I haven't finished yet. It goes on to say that she's the wife of Sir George Latimer, second secretary to the Foreign Minister.

**PENNY.** You mean the woman could be married to one of Hugo's friends?

**RALPH.** I'd say it's practically a certainty, wouldn't you?

**PENNY.** I suppose so. What should we do?

**RALPH.** What do you mean? What could we do?

**PENNY.** Well, we could phone to let Hugo know.

**RALPH.** Why?

**PENNY.** To give him advance notice so it won't be such a shock when somebody tells him.

**RALPH.** No. He'd be asked how he found out. Then he'd say a friend in Somerset had phoned to tell him and be accused of gossiping about the Latimers with people who didn't even know them.

**PENNY.** You could ask him to pretend he hadn't already heard about it when somebody told him.

**RALPH.** Not a hope. Hugo's totally incapable of telling a lie. Always has been. Whenever he tries, he blushes bright red and starts to babble or stutter.

**PENNY.** So what are we going to do, then?

**RALPH.** Nothing. He'll find out when he gets to the office tomorrow.

**PENNY.** That seems awfully cruel.

**RALPH.** Cruel? Why on earth is it cruel?

**PENNY.** Not to warn him.

**RALPH.** Look, I've already explained that …

**PENNY.** No, not about Lady Latimer.

**RALPH.** Not about … Then what do you mean?

**PENNY.** About …Sybil and … that shawl … my shawl.

**RALPH.** What about your shawl?

**PENNY.** Well, I lent it to her.

**RALPH.** I know. So what?

**PENNY.** I can't help worrying that … something similar could … oh, I know you'll think I'm silly, but the paper said that woman had been strangled with her scarf and she's a famous designer who made a name by creating clothes in black and white.

**RALPH.** What's that got to do with Hugo and telling him about a traffic accident?

**PENNY.** Well, that man, Janos, kept some of the wool from that sheep you killed so his wife - his woman, I mean – could knit a scarf. A black one. Suppose it was that scarf she was wearing and it choked her?

**RALPH.** Oh, come on! A famous designer isn't going to buy her outfits from some gypsy!

**PENNY.** You never know! It could be some kind of fashion trend or statement. It would be a one-of -a-kind accessory. That's what designers go for.

**RALPH.** How did the scarf get to her? You're being ridiculous!

**PENNY.** No! Remember that Hugo said that George Latimer was into the occult. Maybe he was trying out some black magic that went wrong. Success for his wife's career or something.

**RALPH.** I don't believe what I'm hearing! How could …

**PENNY.** Just listen to me! What if the black scarf was an instrument of evil he'd conjured up to make people want to buy her clothes and …

**RALPH.** Or maybe it was a terrorist sign to tell secret agents to carry out a suicide bomb attack on the Foreign Office.

**PENNY.** Let me finish! His spell could have gone wrong so that the black scarf became a sort of magnet for …

**RALPH.** We don't even know that the scarf was black. Perhaps it was red and part of a Communist plot to destroy the British fashion industry.

**PENNY.** Why won't you listen to me?

**RALPH.** Because you're being stupid, that's why!

**PENNY.** I'm not stupid!

**RALPH.** Hysterical, then.

**PENNY.** I'm not hysterical either!

***PENNY bursts into tears. After a few moments, RALPH begins to comfort her.***

**RALPH.** All right, Penny. I'm sorry. Come on. Don't be so upset.

**PENNY.** Ralph, I'm scared!

**RALPH.** Scared of what?

**PENNY.** Of … of my … of that shawl!

**RALPH.** The shawl? But that's silly!

**PENNY.** I know it's silly, but I can't help it. I'm terrified of what it will do to Sybil.

**RALPH.** Why should it do anything to Sybil? And what could it do?

**PENNY.** I've no idea. But when I gave it to her today, I suddenly had a premonition, a terrifying chill that gripped me. There was no warning. It hit me the instant I touched the shawl. One moment I was warm, chatting and laughing with Sybil, the next I was freezing and paralyzed with fear. I almost told her not to take it.

**RALPH.** Did Sybil notice anything?

**PENNY.** Yes, she asked me what was wrong.

**RALPH.** So what did you say? Anything about the shawl?

**PENNY.** No. I decided that she'd had enough terror in her life – all those nightmares and everything – so I wouldn't throw any more at her. I wish now that I'd told her how I was feeling about the thing.

**RALPH.** But why? Nothing's happened to her.

**PENNY.** Not as far as we know. But something's happened to that other woman, hasn't it? To Lady Latimer.

**RALPH.** There's no connection between …

**PENNY.**  Of course there is! Her husband and Sybil's are friends and he's involved in evil spirits and she was choked by her scarf and she wears black clothes and my shawl is black and that dreadful gypsy wanted you to give him your black wool for a scarf and …

***PENNY bursts into tears again.***

**RALPH.**  Oh, Penny, please don't get so upset! It's all a coincidence.

**PENNY.**  I can't help being upset. I just can't believe that what happened to Lady Latimer isn't connected with Sybil and the shawl I lent her.

**RALPH.**  No, it isn't! You're imagining everything.

**PENNY.**  You can't see what's in my mind. Every time I think of Sybil, I see her in awful pain with that evil gypsy looming over her, ready to pounce on her and strangle the life out of her.

**RALPH.**  Now you're being really silly. Janos has disappeared completely, vanished from the face of the earth. You'll never see him again and Sybil will be fine.

**PENNY.**  Shouldn't we at least phone them in a couple of hours, once they've had time to get home. To check that nothing's happened to them.

**RALPH.**  No. If anything happens, we'll hear about it.

**PENNY.**  Who from?

**RALPH.**  If something happens to Sybil, Ralph will call..

**PENNY.**  And what if they have a crash that kills both of them on the way home?

**RALPH.**  Then we'll hear about it on TV or read it in the paper. And what does it really matter? We couldn't do anything about it. Look, we're leaving next week for a long holiday. You'll be able to relax and forget all about it.

When we get back, Sybil and Hugo will come round to see us and we'll all have a good laugh about it.

53

*The LIGHTS fade.*

## ACT II, Scene 2.

### *An afternoon in January*

**RALPH.** Isn't it good to be home? And just look at the garden! Not the least bit of damage to any of the hedges.

**PENNY.** It certainly is nice to have you not cursing about that black ram. And to be back with Morrison's plain, wholesome home cooking after all the rich food!

**RALPH.** Well, I'm not sure I agree with you there.

**PENNY.** Ralph, she's a wonderful cook.

**RALPH.** Oh, yes I agree about that. But when I think of those meals on the cruise ship, my tongue just hangs out.

**PENNY.** Yes, and so would your stomach if you ate like that for much longer. Anyway, I appreciate her food, even if you don't.

**RALPH.** But I do! I was only having a wistful moment of memory.

**PENNY.** Make sure she doesn't hear your wistful moments. I've asked her to serve tea in here.

**RALPH.** A bit early, isn't it? It's not half past three yet.

**PENNY.** I know, but it's been a long day, what with the flight delay and the crowded train from Paddington, then just missing that bus. I could have killed that driver.

**RALPH.** Yes, he obviously saw us clearly. And he knew we couldn't move any faster with that luggage.

### *ENTER MORRISON with a tray full of letters.*

**MORRISON.** Excuse me, Madame, but I thought you might like to look at the post while you're waiting for your tea. It won't be long.

**PENNY.** Thank you, Morrison. Good idea.

**RALPH.** Look at the stack we've got!

**PENNY.** Most of it's probably Christmas cards.

**RALPH.**  Put it over there, Morrison, please. We'll look at it later.

**MORRISON.**  Yes, sir.

*MORRISON takes the letters to a table, shelf, etc., then exits.*

**RALPH.**  Isn't it nice to see the hedge undamaged and the garden not trampled by sheep?

**PENNY.**  Yes, dear, it is. We already agreed on that. I wonder if Inspector Barclay has got anywhere with his enquiries?

**RALPH.**  No idea, but let's not spoil the memory of a lovely holiday by worrying about it. He'll get in touch with us if he needs us.

**PENNY.**  I suppose so. And I wonder if Hugo and Sybil are both all right.

**RALPH.**  Same answer and same solution.

**PENNY.**  I'm still a bit worried about that shawl and whether …

*ENTER MORRISON.*

**MORRISON.**  Excuse me, sir. That policeman is here and would like to see you.

**RALPH.**  Policeman? You mean Inspector Barclay?

**MORRISON.**  Yes, sir.

**PENNY.**  Ask him to come in, then, Morrison.

**MORRISON.**  Yes, Madame.

*EXIT MORRISON.*

**RALPH.**  I wonder what he wants.

**PENNY.**  We'll soon find out.

**RALPH.**  Maybe they've caught that gypsy.

**PENNY.**  Or maybe they've found our missing meat and caught the thief, so it had nothing to do with Janos.

### *ENTER MORRISON, with BARCLAY.*

**RALPH.**  Inspector! Good to see you again.

**PENNY.**  We've only just got back from our holiday.

**BARCLAY.**  Yes, I know. My sergeant saw you get out of your taxi as he drove past. He knew I wanted to see you as soon as possible, so he called the station and I drove over straight away.

**RALPH.**  What's the rush, inspector?

**BARCLAY.**  There've been some developments in the case. Have you got that shawl back yet?

 Xp No. We were just talking about it when you got here. But did our meat turn up?

**BARCLAY.**  No, which means that the shawl is our only connection to the gypsy.

**RALPH.**  What are these new developments?

**BARCLAY.**  That black hen turned out to be a cock and is terrorizing the people who got it.

**PENNY.**  How?

**BARCLAY.**  For a start, it killed off the other three cocks in the flock so it had no rivals. Then every egg laid by the hens produced a chick that was black instead of yellow and turned out to be as aggressive as the cock was. The wife decided to get rid of the thing and was going to wring its neck, but every black chicken in the flock went for her. She was so badly pecked that the hospital staff thought she might be blind in one eye. She recovered, but they daren't go near the birds any one more. You can see why I want to get hold of that shawl. It's the only clue we have.

**PENNY.** Ralph, why don't you phone Hugo and Sybil to ask them if they can get it back to us? Explain why it's so urgent.

**RALPH.** I will, yes.



**PENNY.** Will it be helpful once you get it, inspector?

**BARCLAY.** I don't know, to tell you the truth. The forensic team won't be able to get as much as they would from the wrapping paper, I'm sure. There won't be any chance of pulling his fingerprints or DNA traces from it, for instance, but they'll find out the breed of sheep. If it's an unusual one, we might possibly be able to pinpoint the location it came from and get hold of this gypsy that way.

**PENNY.** Will anybody there know him if he's the normal type of gypsy?

**BARCLAY.** Wandering around the country, buying and selling things to make a living, you mean?

**PENNY.** Yes.

**BARCLAY.** Ah, that's the question, isn't it? We'll just have to hope we get some good luck there.

*ENTER RALPH.*

**RALPH.** There's no reply. They must be out. I left a message on their machine.

**PENNY.** Are they all right, do you think?

**RALPH.** Of course they are! Hugo's probably at the office and Sybil's out shopping, I expect.

**PENNY.** Ralph, it's Sunday afternoon. Hugo won't be working.

**RALPH.** Maybe something urgent came up. Or they could have gone out to visit friends, gone for tea, something like that. They'll call back when they get home and listen to my message.

**BARCLAY.** Yes and when they do, please contact me at once to let me know. I'll give you my card.

**RALPH.**  Thanks. I'll put it by the phone.

**BARCLAY.**  You can tell them we'll arrange for it to be collected and driven here to save them the bother of coming themselves.

**RALPH.**  I will.

**BARCLAY.**  Good. Well I think that's all I can do for now, so I'll get back to the station and wait to hear from you.

**PENNY.**  Goodbye, inspector.

**_EXIT BARCLAY and RALPH. PENNY picks up a newspaper. After a few moments, RALPH returns._**

**PENNY.**  Ralph, I'm really worried about Hugo and Sybil.

**RALPH.**  Why? Just because they're not home on a Sunday afternoon doesn't mean there's any problem for them.

**PENNY.**  I know that, but I've had a niggling feeling at the back of my mind ever since we last saw them.

**RALPH.**  What, even when we were on holiday?

**PENNY.**  Yes, it kept coming back to me.

**RALPH.**  And I thought you were enjoying yourself.

**PENNY.**  I was, but the disturbing thoughts kept intruding.

**RALPH.**  I hope you're not going to get in the same state as you were before we went away.

**PENNY.**  I'll try not to.

**RALPH.**  You've got to get your mind under control before your emotions get hold of you.

**PENNY.**  I know, and I'll try my best, but I hope Inspector Barclay can catch that Janos before anybody else is killed by him. I can't get the image of Lady Latimer being dragged along by that car out of my mind.

**RALPH.** Look, this is exactly what I meant when I said you should get your mind under control. There's absolutely no evidence to suggest any connection between that gypsy and Lady Latimer.

**PENNY.** All right, all right, but I can't …

***ENTER MORRISON.***

**MORRISON.** Excuse me, Madame, but …

***She is pushed out of the way as a wild-looking HUGO bursts in, with a parcel in his hands.***

**RALPH.** Hugo, hello. What are you doing here? I was trying to phone you a few minutes ago. Inspector Barclay was hoping to …

**HUGO.** I've come to bring this thing back to you.

**PENNY.** We've only just got back from our holiday. You're lucky to catch us.

**HUGO.** So Morrison tells me.

**RALPH.** What is it?

***HUGO tears the parcel open to reveal the shawl.***

**PENNY.** It's the shawl!

**RALPH.** You shouldn't have rushed to get it back to us. We don't need it in any hurry.

**HUGO.** I wanted to get rid of the damned thing!

**PENNY.** Is Sybil here with you?

**HUGO.** No, Sybil is not here with me.

**RALPH.** Why didn't she come with you? She's well, I hope, isn't she?

**HUGO.** No, Sybil is not well. Sybil is dead.

**RALPH.** What?

**PENNY.** Dead?

**HUGO.**  Yes, dead.

**PENNY.**  What happened?

**HUGO.**  She was strangled to death. Murdered by this shawl.

***HUGO hurls the shawl to the ground.***

**RALPH.**  How?

**HUGO.**  I think she was getting ready to go out. Looking for Tumkins. Somebody's stolen him. She was putting the shawl on and it must have got stuck. The autopsy report said she'd got tangled in it and must have got into a panic. It got pulled tight and cut off her air supply. Remember how she was when you let her try it on, Penny?

**PENNY.**  Yes, but …

**HUGO.**  Accidental death, the coroner said. But we know differently, don't we? She was murdered, deliberately strangled by that shawl.

**PENNY.**  You can't believe that, Hugo. It's just an inanimate object, a piece of knitting. It can't do anybody any harm.

**HUGO.**  Can it not? Really? Then perhaps you'd like to try putting it on, would you?

**PENNY.**  No, I … It's too … warm in here. It would be very … uncomfortable.

**HUGO.**  Put it on, I said. And without any help standing by when you want to take it off.

**PENNY.**  No, I'd rather …

**HUGO.**  Come on! Here, I'll hold your arm and help you to get it on.

**PENNY.**  Hugo, please! Don't! You're hurting me.

**RALPH.**  Come off it, Hugo! That's enough. You've made your point and we're very sorry about Sybil, but …

**HUGO.**  Oh, you're sorry, are you? Well, that's a great consolation, but I want Penny to know what it feels like when her shawl chokes her to death.

*HUGO grabs the tray, scattering all the letters and begins to attack RALPH with it.*

**PENNY.**  He's insane! Morrison, phone 999 and get the police here. Better still, call Barclay. His number's right there, beside the phone.

*EXIT MORRISON.*

**HUGO.**  Now you can learn how to mind your own business.

*HUGO swings the tray and strikes RALPH in the solar plexus. RALPH doubles up and sinks to his knees on the floor. HUGO drops the tray and returns to the task of forcing PENNY into the shawl.*

**HUGO.**  Your turn again, Penny.
**PENNY.**  Ralph! Please! Help me! Let me go, Hugo.

*HUGO continues trying to force PENNY into the shawl during the following speech.*

**HUGO.**  Not until you get this shawl on and find out how it feels when the garment wraps itself round your throat and slowly chokes you to death while you struggle to escape but can't get away and you feel the breath being squeezed out of you and you can't suck any air in to replace it and you know you can do nothing to save your life.

*ENTER MORRISON.*

**MORRISON.**  Let her go! The police are on their way to stop you.

**HUGO.**  By the time they get here she'll be dead. The police won't get here in four minutes and that's all it takes before you're dead without air to breathe.

**MORRISON.**  Then they'll arrest you for murdering her.

**HUGO.**  Really? She murdered my wife and I don't see any signs of the police arresting her.

*MORRISON grapples with him in an attempt to rescue PENNY. He flings her away and she collapses into a chair, sobbing. HUGO returns to PENNY.*

**HUGO.**  Will you get this shawl on, or do I have to choke the life out of you with my bare hands?

*RALPH struggles to his feet and picks up the tray, then swings it at HUGO, striking him a glancing blow. The two men begin to fight furiously. PENNY sinks into a chair and tries weakly to free her arms from the shawl.*

*The French window opens suddenly and JÁNOS ENTERS.*

**MORRISON.**  It's the gypsy man!

*Both women begin to scream. JÁNOS points towards them.*

**JÁNOS.**  Vridutz!

*They immediately stop screaming. The two men haven't noticed him and continue fighting.*

**PENNY.**  Ralph! Hugo! It's Janos! He's here!
**JÁNOS.**  My name, he is *János*, not Janos.

*RALPH and HUGO stop fighting.*

**RALPH.**  What? Who? You! The police are looking for you. They want to question you about that black chicken.
**JÁNOS.**  The police? Hah! They are of no interest to me, your police.
**RALPH.**  Really? We'll see about that when they arrive. What are you doing here, anyway?
**JÁNOS.**  I come to take back my shawl.
**RALPH.**  Do you? I think the police might refuse to let you.
**HUGO.**  You're not taking it. Not until Penny has been strangled by it.
**RALPH.**  No! Get it off her, right now.
**JÁNOS.**  Stop to fight! Sit!
**HUGO.**  Not while she's still alive.
**RALPH.**  Not until this maniac stops trying to murder my wife.
**JÁNOS.**  Sit! There!

*He points to the sofa. RALPH and HUGO instantly drop into it, side by side.*

**JÁNOS.**  Now I take shawl. Is needed for other persons. Come here, woman.

*PENNY stands and moves to him, seemingly in a trance. He begins to get her arms untangled from the sleeves.*

**HUGO.**  Leave it on her, I've told you.

**RALPH.**  Take it off her and wait for the police. We've just phoned them. They'll be here any minute.

**JÁNOS.**  Is enough talk!

*He points to RALPH.*

**JÁNOS.**  You, take hand and put around throat of other.

*RALPH does so. JÁNOS points to HUGO.*

**JÁNOS.**  You! Do same thing.

*HUGO grasps RALPH by the throat.*

**JÁNOS.**  Is good. Now, both. Put other hand behind neck of other man.

*RALPH and HUGO obey in a trance.*

**JÁNOS.**  This is very good. Now, squeeze with all hands.

*They do so and both begin choking.*

**JÁNOS.**  Is good. Now I need shawl. Give to me. I need for getting more woman.

*JÁNOS helps to remove SYBIL'S arms from the shawl, with some difficulty.*

**JÁNOS.**  Now, who is telephoning to police?

**MORRISON.**  I did, sir. I called Inspector Barclay.

**JÁNOS.**  Ah, so you know private telephone number of this policeman, yes?

**MORRISON.**  No, sir. But he left a card with the number on it.

**JÁNOS.**  So you give to me this card.

**MORRISON.**  I haven't got it, sir. It's beside the phone, out in the hallway.

**JÁNOS.**  This is evidence. I must find and remove, take away with me.

*JÁNOS exits to the hall.*

*BARCLAY ENTERS from the garden, through the French windows.*

**BARCLAY.**  I couldn't get in at the front door. What's the trouble you're having with Sir Hugo Neville, Mrs. Barnes? The call sounded urgent, so I came here at once to find out what …

*He sees the two bodies on the sofa, not moving.*

**BARCLAY.**  What the hell's going on here?

*BARCLAY rushes across to the sofa and tries to break the grip of the two men on each other's throat.*

**BARCLAY.**  No pulse for either of them.

*ENTER JÁNOS.*

**BARCLAY.**  What's going on here? Oh, wait a minute. Are you that gypsy, Janos? We've been wanting to find you for quite a while now.

**JÁNOS.**  My name, he is *János*, not Janos.

**BARCLAY.**   Well, whatever your name is, you're coming to the station with me for questioning.

**JÁNOS.**  No.

**BARCLAY.**  What do you mean, no? I said …

**JÁNOS.**  Sit! Here, on chair.

***BARCLAY sits where he is told.***

**JÁNOS.**  Here you will sleep until morning. You will awaken at eight o'clock, not earlier. Do you understand?

**BARCLAY.**  Yes. I understand.

**JÁNOS.**   You will remember nothing about what happens here. You will find the bodies of two men who have killed each other. You will find no sign of anyone else. You will telephone to your policemen to come, but you will not be able to explain why you are here. You will also not tell why telephone to you happens and what you say to it. Do you understand?

**BARCLAY.**  Yes. I understand.

**JÁNOS.**  That is good. Sleep now.

***BARCLAY immediately falls asleep in the chair.***

**JÁNOS.**  Good. Now, I take shawl. I must give to people who have trouble with black sheeps. Also, I need more womans. I take two of you. You will forget all memory. You will take care of my new cat. He is very good cat, all black everywhere. You will knit and sew for me. You will make other shawls. You will not remember having other life. For rest of time, you will serve me. Is good, yes?

**PENNY.**  Is good, yes.

**MORRISON.**  Is good, yes.

**JÁNOS.**  So, we go now. *Come.*

*EXIT JÁNOS, followed by PENNY and MORRISON, leaving BARCLAY asleep in the chair, with the bodies of RALPH and HUGO still holding each other by the throat as the LIGHTS fade.*